# Little Things

by Amy Jo • illustrated by Amy Cartwright

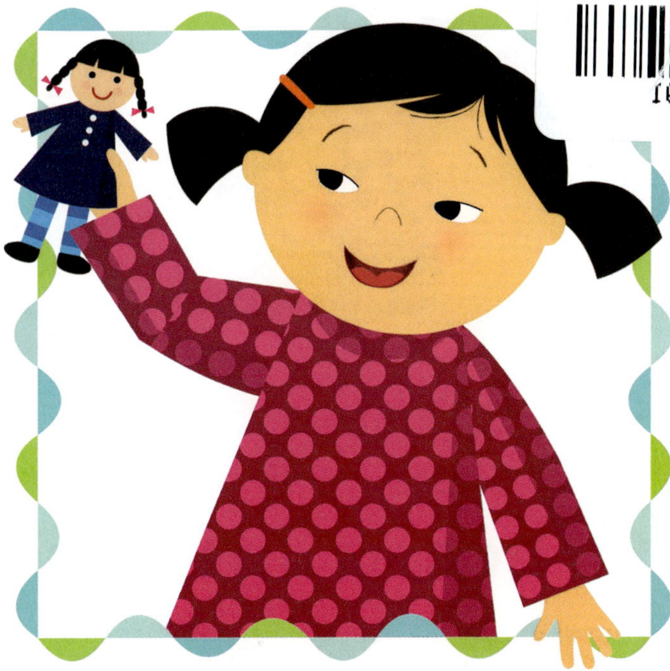

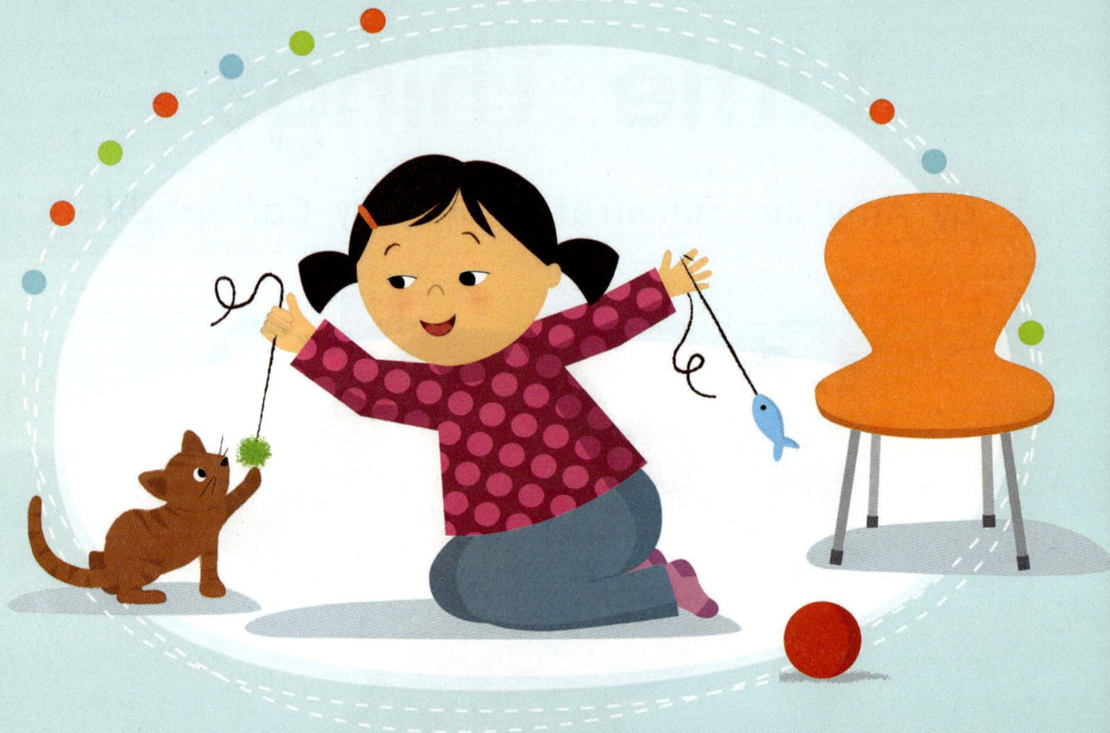

Jan has a little cat.

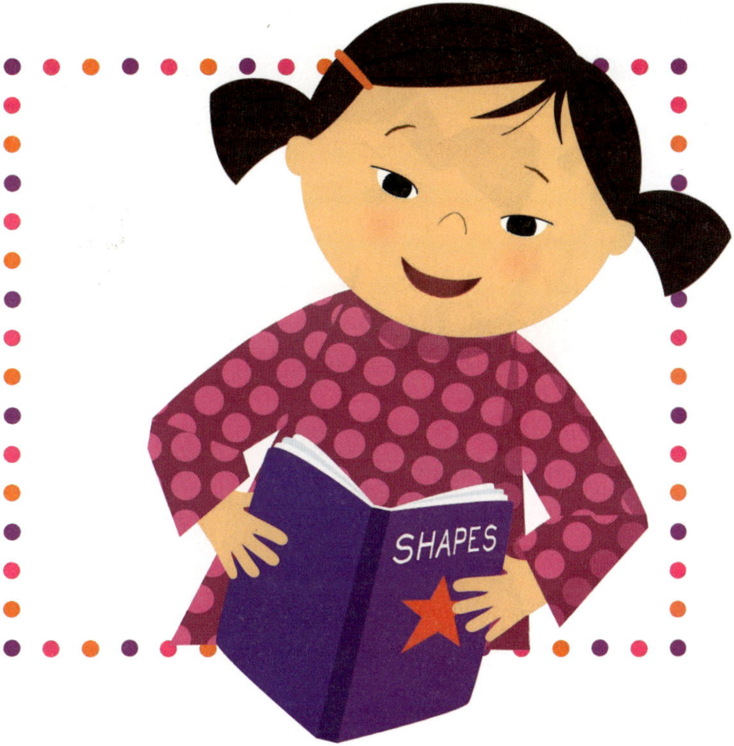


Jan has a little book.

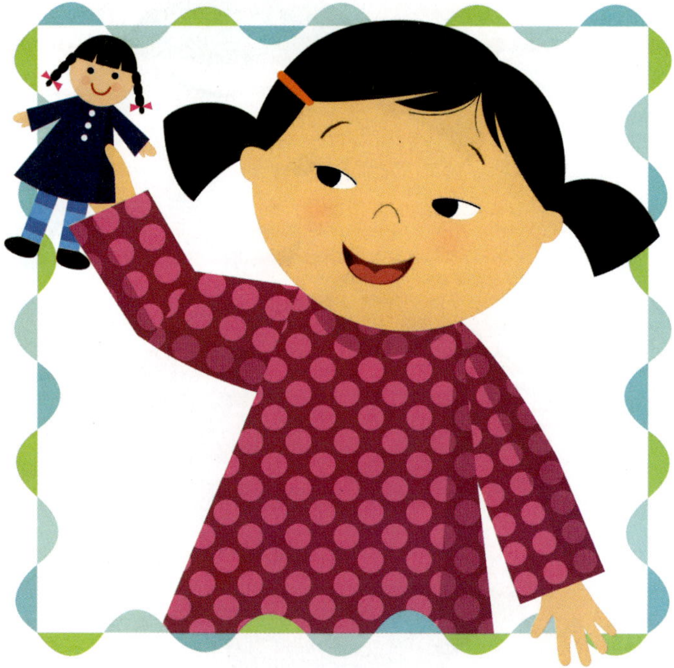

Jan has a little doll.

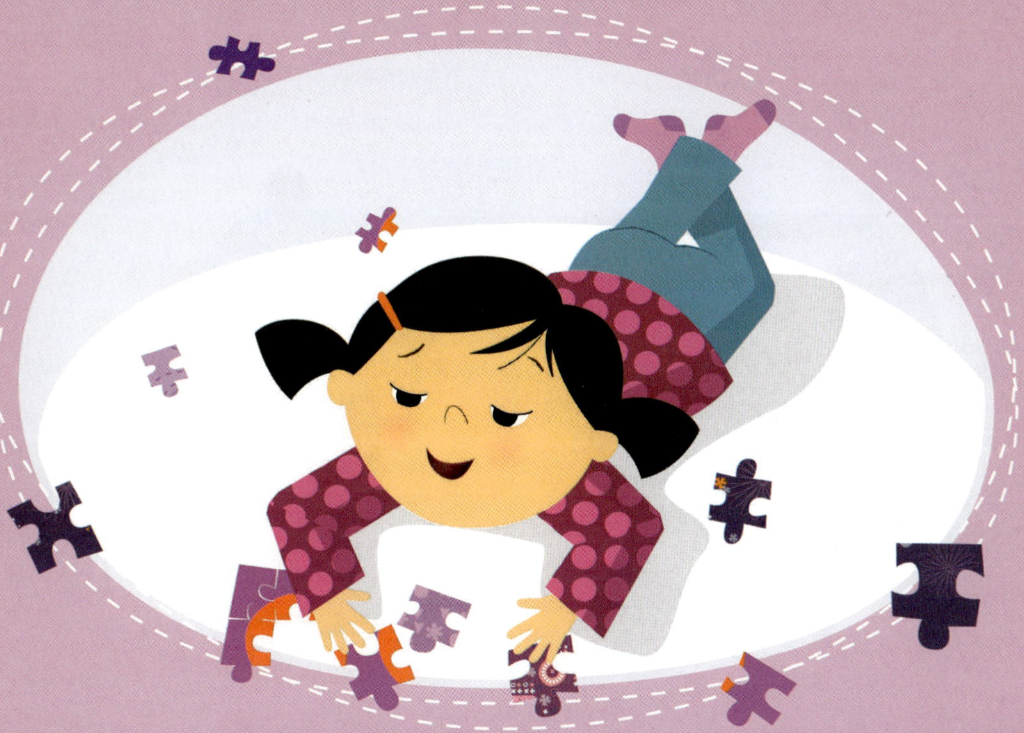

Jan has a little game.

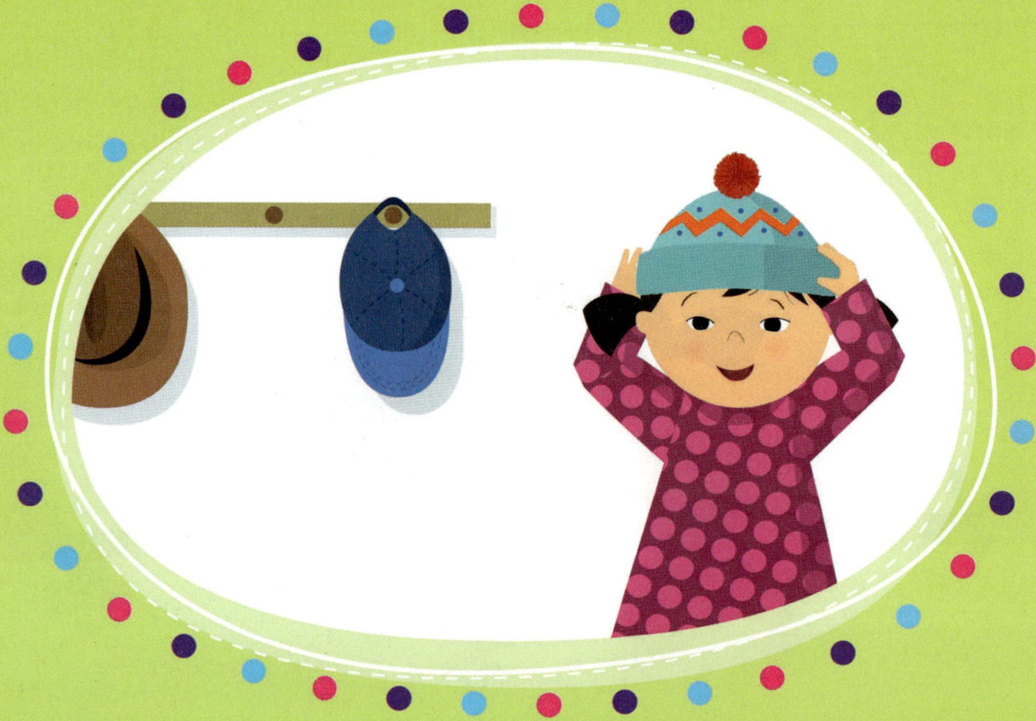

Jan has a little hat.

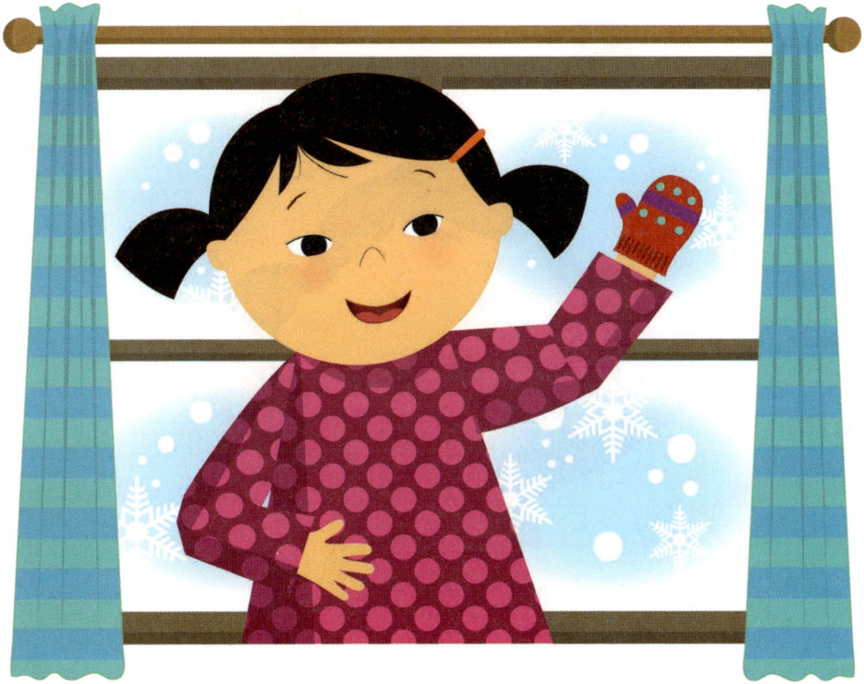

Jan has a little mitten.

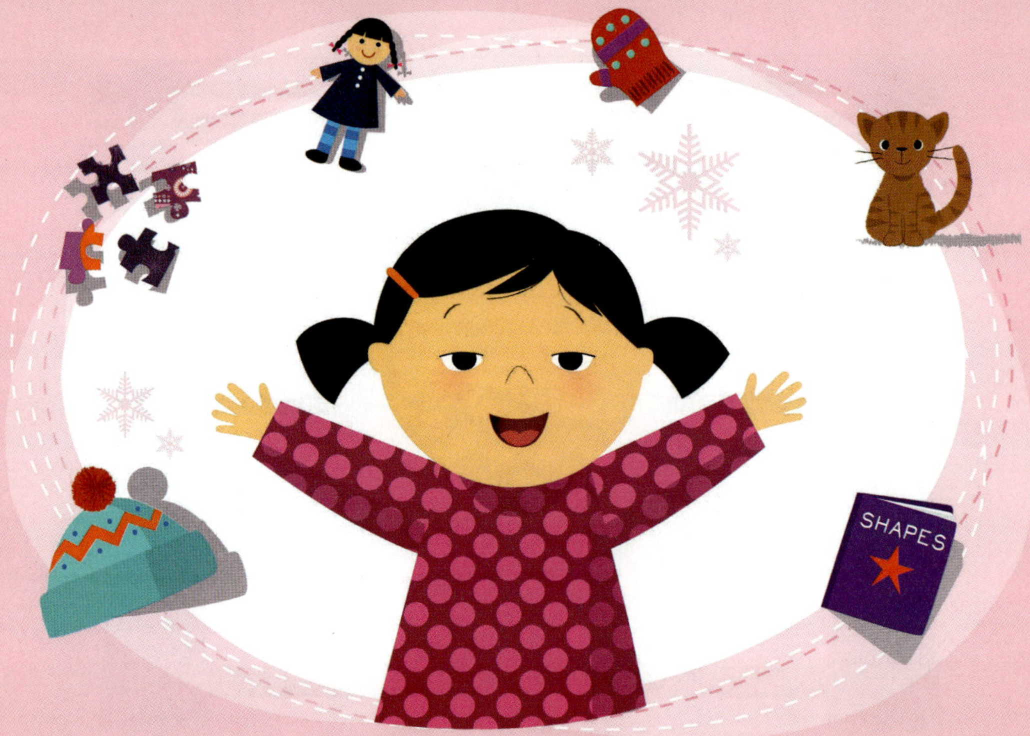


Jan has little things.